D1243517

Roald Dahl

Rennay Craats

www.av2books.com

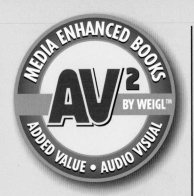

AV² provides enriched content that supplements and complements this book. Weigl's AV² books strive to create inspired learning and engage young minds in a total learning experience.

Your AV² Media Enhanced books come alive with...

Audio
Listen to sections of the book read aloud.

Video
Watch informative video clips.

Embedded Weblinks
Gain additional information for research.

Try This!
Complete activities and hands-on experiments.

Key Words
Study vocabulary, and complete a matching word activity.

Quizzes
Test your knowledge.

Slide Show
View images and captions, and prepare a presentation.

... and much, much more!

Go to **www.av2books.com**, and enter this book's unique code.

BOOK CODE

A208869

AV² by Weigl brings you media enhanced books that support active learning.

Published by AV² by Weigl
350 5th Avenue, 59th Floor
New York, NY 10118

Website: www.weigl.com www.av2books.com

Library of Congress Control Number: 2013953130

ISBN 978-1-4896-0676-1 (hardcover)
ISBN 978-1-4896-0677-8 (softcover)
ISBN 978-1-4896-0678-5 (single user eBook)
ISBN 978-1-4896-0679-2 (multi-user eBook)

Printed in the United States of America, in North Mankato, Minnesota
1 2 3 4 5 6 7 8 9 0 18 17 16 15 14

012014
WEP301113

Senior Editor: Heather Kissock
Design: Terry Paulhus

Weigl acknowledges Getty Images, Alamy, Newscom, Jan Baldwin, and The Roald Dahl Foundation as its primary photo suppliers for this title.

Contents

Introducing Roald Dahl

Children love reading author Roald Dahl's books. For nearly fifty years, Roald wrote exciting stories about cruel villains and the brave children who seek revenge on them. His zany characters delight readers of all ages. Roald has written books about cruel witches, dangerous gremlins, and children with superpowers. The unexpected twists and turns of a Roald Dahl book keep readers turning the pages. Many of Roald Dahl's readers are devoted fans.

The 2005 film of *Charlie and the Chocolate Factory* gave new life to Roald's vibrant imagination and quirky characters contained in the book of the same name.

Writers are often inspired to record the stories of people who lead interesting lives. The story of another person's life is called a biography. A biography can tell the story of any person, from authors such as Roald Dahl, to inventors, presidents, and sports stars.

When writing a biography, authors must first collect information about their subject. This information may come from a book about the person's life, a news article about one of his or her accomplishments, or a review of his or her work. Libraries and the internet will have much of this information. Most biographers will also interview their subjects. Personal accounts provide a great deal of information and a unique point of view. When some basic details about the person's life have been collected, it is time to begin writing a biography.

As you read about Roald Dahl, you will be introduced to the important parts of a biography. Use these tips and the examples provided to learn how to write about an author or any other remarkable person.

📖 Trolls are common in Scandinavian folktales. In most stories, they can be found living in caves, mountains, or isolated woodland areas.

As a young child, Roald loved to read. His bedroom was filled with books and his mind was filled with stories. Roald and his sisters would gather around their mother to listen to tales of trolls and other creatures found in Norwegian **mythology**. When he was alone, Roald's active imagination worked overtime. However, the idea of writing stories did not occur to Roald until he was much older. Roald began writing in his twenties. Once he started, there was no stopping him.

Early Life

Roald Dahl was born in Llandaff, Wales on September 13, 1916. His parents, Sofie and Harald, were of Norwegian descent. The Dahl family experienced a tragic loss when Roald was only 3 years old. Astri, Roald's oldest sister, died of **appendicitis**. The following year, Harald caught **pneumonia**. Sadly, he died shortly after. Although these were difficult times, Sofie remained strong. Roald Dahl remembered his mother as a woman who gave him a wonderful feeling of security.

As a young boy, Roald went to Llandaff Cathedral School. On his way to and from school, he enjoyed passing the candy shop. Roald and his friends would gaze at the mouth-watering sweets through the window. Sometimes, they would pool their money to buy a treat. The store owner did not like the children hanging around. As a prank, one day the boys hid a dead mouse inside one of the candy jars. The owner was furious when she discovered it.

"The writer for children must be a jokey sort of a fellow . . . he must like simple tricks and jokes and riddles and other childish things. He must be unconventional and inventive. He must have a really first-class plot."
—*Roald Dahl*

As a child, Roald spent his summers with his grandparents in Oslo, Norway.

Soon, the school's headmaster found out about the prank. He whacked the boys with a cane as the shop owner cheered. Roald's mother was very angry about her son's punishment. She moved him to a boarding school called St. Peter's.

Roald did not enjoy boarding school either. Roald tried to stay out of trouble, but trouble seemed to find him. He was very homesick, and he longed for summer to arrive. Every summer, he joined his family for a vacation in Norway.

When Roald was 13 years old, he attended a school called Repton, in Derbyshire, England. Repton was close to Cadbury's chocolate factory. Roald and his friends were allowed to sample the new chocolate bars prepared in the factory. The author's love for chocolate and candy lasted a lifetime. It even inspired one of his best-selling children's stories, *Charlie and the Chocolate Factory*.

The Cadbury chocolate factory is located in Birmingham, England. The company has been making chocolate for more than 250 years.

A person's early years have a strong influence on his or her future. Parents, teachers, and friends can have a large impact on how a person thinks, feels, and behaves. These effects are strong enough to last throughout childhood, and often a person's lifetime.

In order to write about a person's early life, biographers must find answers to the following questions.

1 Where and when was the person born?

2 What is known about the person's family and friends?

3 Did the person grow up in unusual circumstances?

Growing Up

Roald Dahl was a great athlete, but his academic abilities were not as strong. Although he enjoyed reading, he was not a good writer according to his teachers. They told him that his **vocabulary** was small and his sentences were poorly structured. One of his teachers was frustrated with Roald's habit of writing the opposite of what he meant.

> Roald wanted to experience adventures similar to those in the books he read.

However, some teachers recognized his artistic talents. Roald could draw well, and was also an excellent photographer. He even built his own darkroom at the school.

By the time Roald graduated from high school, he was more than ready to leave. Roald decided that he never wanted to be a student again. He did not attend university or college. Instead, he worked and traveled. Roald wanted to experience adventures similar to those in the books he read. Roald looked for a job that would allow him to travel to other countries.

Get to Know Wales

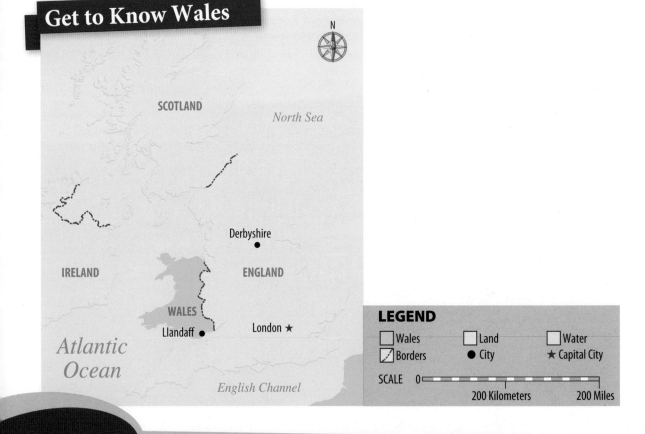

SCOTLAND

North Sea

Derbyshire

IRELAND

ENGLAND

WALES

Llandaff

London ★

Atlantic Ocean

English Channel

LEGEND

| ☐ Wales | ☐ Land | ☐ Water |
| ▨ Borders | ● City | ★ Capital City |

SCALE   0 ⌷—————————————
200 Kilometers   200 Miles

Roald got a job working for the Shell Oil Company in East Africa. Roald had many adventures. He learned to speak **Swahili**, contracted a disease called malaria, and went on safaris where he saw wild animals. When Roald saw a lion fling a woman onto the ground, he wrote about it in an African newspaper. This marked the beginning of his writing career. Roald felt a strong urge to write about his incredible experiences.

While Roald was in Africa, World War II began. Roald enlisted in the Royal Air Force (RAF) as a fighter pilot. During his first mission, he crashed in the desert in Libya. Roald broke his nose and fractured his skull. This left him blind for weeks. For five months, he recovered in a navy hospital. When he recovered, he went back to battle in World War II.

Writing About Growing Up

Some people know what they want to achieve in life from a very young age. Others do not decide until much later. In any case, it is important for biographers to discuss when and how their subjects make these decisions. Using the information they collect, biographers try to answer the following questions about their subjects' paths in life.

1 Who had the most influence on the person?

2 Did he or she receive assistance from others?

3 Did the person have a positive attitude?

✍ Roald Dahl was 6 feet, 6 inches tall. His entire head stuck out of the cockpit when he was seated in most fighter planes.

Developing Skills

Eventually, Roald's injuries made flying impossible. The RAF stationed him in the United States, where he worked at the British Embassy in Washington, DC. At the embassy, Roald met a well-known American writer, C. S. Forester. He asked Roald to write about his World War II experiences. Roald eagerly accepted. He wrote down his personal feelings about the war on paper. Roald's notes were published in the *Saturday Evening Post*. Soon, Roald's stories began appearing in many highly respected magazines across the United States.

"Children's books are harder to write. It's tougher to keep a child interested . . . the child knows the television is in the next room. It's tough to hold a child, but it's a lovely thing to try to do."
—*Roald Dahl*

The *Saturday Evening Post* was originally called the *Pennsylvania Gazette*. The magazine has been publishing since the 1700s.

Roald's first book, *The Gremlins*, was published in 1943. It was a children's story about furry, trouble-making creatures. The book was **adapted** from a movie script. Although *The Gremlins* was published, the movie deal fell through. The movie was finally produced forty years later, in 1984.

In 1945, Roald returned to England. He wrote short stories for adults. He was praised for his interesting plots, attention to detail, and surprise endings. Roald decided to move to the publishing center of the United States—New York City. Roald met many interesting people there, including movie actress Patricia Neal. The two fell in love and were married in 1953. The following year, they had a daughter, Olivia. Over the next few years, the Dahl family grew.

✍ In the 1984 film version of *Gremlins*, a boy receives a pet called a Mogwai for Christmas. When he does not care for it properly, the creature produces evil offspring that wreak havoc on the boy's hometown.

Every remarkable person has skills and traits that make him or her noteworthy. Some people have natural talent, while others practice diligently. For most, it is a combination of the two. One of the most important things that a biographer can do is to tell the story of how the subject developed his or her talents.

1 What was the person's education?

2 What was the person's first job or work experience?

3 What obstacles did the person overcome?

Timeline of Roald Dahl

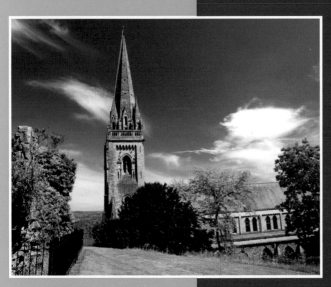

1916
Roald Dahl was born in Llandaff, Wales on September 13.

1953
Roald marries American actress Patricia Neal.

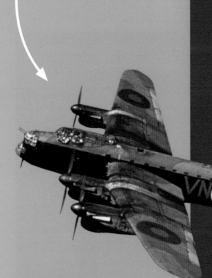

1939
Roald joins the Royal Air Force as a fighter pilot.

1943
Roald writes his first children's novel, *The Gremlins*.

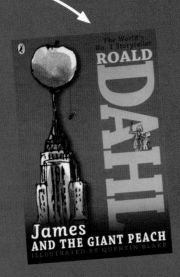

1962
James and the Giant Peach
is published.

1964
*Charlie and the Chocolate
Factory* is published.

1990
Roald dies on
November 23.

1988
Matilda is published.

Early Achievements

Roald spent nine months writing *James and the Giant Peach* before turning it over to his publisher, Alfred Knopf. Alfred was thrilled that the book contained such original ideas. Before it even hit bookstore shelves, Roald began writing his next book. It was about a mysterious chocolate factory. Little did he know that this book would make him a celebrity. However, readers could not get a copy of *Charlie and the Chocolate Factory* right away. Roald's family faced many tragedies, which delayed the **publication** of the book.

"A story starts always with a tiny little seed of an idea, a little germ, and that even doesn't come very easily . . . When I do get a good one, mind you, I quickly write it down so that I won't forget it, because it disappears otherwise, rather like a dream." —*Roald Dahl*

In 1960, Roald's son, Theo, was seriously injured when a taxi ran into his baby stroller. Theo survived, but was left with brain damage. Two years after the accident, Roald's oldest daughter, Olivia, died after contracting **measles encephalitis**. This loss crushed the devoted father. Roald was certain that he would never write again.

Roald enjoyed telling his own children stories before tucking them into bed. He once said that he would not have begun writing for children if he had not had children himself.

Despite his personal tragedies, Roald did write again. *Charlie and the Chocolate Factory* was finally published in 1964. Children adored Charlie and the other peculiar characters in the story, making the book a great success. Roald also wrote the movie version of *Charlie and the Chocolate Factory*. The movie was very popular, and book sales skyrocketed after its release in theaters.

Roald's streak of success continued with many more children's books. *Danny the Champion of the World*, *The Twits*, and *The Witches* were all bestsellers. The mysterious chocolate factory reappeared in *Charlie and the Great Glass Elevator* in 1972. *The BFG*, a story about a friendly giant, was published in 1982. It was one of Roald's most popular books. *Matilda*, published in 1988, achieved record-breaking sales. In only six months, the book sold more than 500,000 paperback copies. The award-winning illustrator, Quentin Blake, added his imaginative artwork to many of Dahl's books. Roald Dahl's fantastic stories have been read and treasured by children around the world.

Writing About

Early Achievements

No two people take the same path to success. Some people work very hard for a long time before achieving their goals. Others may take advantage of a fortunate turn of events. Biographers must make special note of the traits and qualities that allow their subjects to succeed.

1 What was the person's most important early success?

2 What processes does the person use in his or her work?

3 Which of the person's traits was most helpful in his or her work?

📖 *Matilda* was adapted for musical theatre by England's Royal Shakespeare Company in 2011. *Matilda the Musical* opened on Broadway in 2013, and went on to win four Tony Awards.

Tricks of the Trade

Everyone writes in a different way. Roald Dahl had particular habits and routines that helped him create his imaginative stories. Read on to learn about Roald's creative writing tips.

Dear Diary

Keeping a journal is a great way to become a better writer. Roald started writing in a secret journal when he was only 8 years old. As an adult, Roald kept his thoughts and ideas in a little red notebook. He always had this book handy. Characters such as Matilda and Charlie were first created in his red notebook.

Schedule Yourself

Often, writers stick to a schedule and write at the same time every day. Roald restricted his writing to only 2 hours at a time. This kept his mind from wandering. Most often, he worked from ten o'clock in the morning until noon. Then he would leave his work area and go about his day. Roald would return to his writing for a couple of hours in the late afternoon.

It is important for writers to have a regular place to write, and a set of tools they are comfortable using. Roald wrote his stories with pencils on yellow legal pads in a small hut at the foot of his garden, which he called his "little nest."

Plot Out the Plot

For fiction writers, the plot is very important. The plot is the outline, or the main events, of the story. When it comes to reading, children can be more **discriminating** than adults. This means that having an interesting plot is very important. Roald Dahl would not begin writing a story until he was completely satisfied with his outline of the plot.

"... there is no artistic reward for a book written for children other than the knowledge that they enjoy it."
—*Roald Dahl*

Writing for Perfection

Every writer has to learn to revise his or her writing. Roald wrote many **drafts** of his books before handing them over to his publisher. Sometimes, he would spend one month rewriting a single page. He wanted to make sure that everything was perfect. Many writers find that revising is the best part of the writing process. Often, a little extra work can make a story shine.

✍ Roald had a great passion for teaching children to become avid readers.

Remarkable Books

R oald's novels are entertaining and enjoyable to read. The following are brief introductions to some of Roald's most-loved stories. Visit your library to explore the fantasy world of Roald Dahl.

Charlie and the Chocolate Factory

Chocolate maker Willy Wonka is known as a strange man. He is rarely seen in public. As a prize in a contest, Willy Wonka invites five winners to visit his mysterious chocolate factory. He hides five golden tickets in his chocolate bars. Those lucky enough to find a ticket win the tour and a lifetime supply of chocolate. Charlie Bucket is a poor boy who desperately wants the prize. One day, Charlie finds money on the street. Instead of giving it to his family for much-needed food, he buys two chocolate bars. Luckily, one bar contains a golden ticket. Charlie is interested in learning about Willy Wonka and his factory. The other winners have greedier intentions: they want to devour as many sweets as possible. Although there are fantastic sights, the visitors' greed soon gets them into trouble.

AWARDS
Charlie and the Chocolate Factory
2000 Millennium Children's Book Award

The World's No. 1 Storyteller
ROALD

Charlie
AND THE CHOCOLATE FACTORY
ILLUSTRATED BY QUENTIN BLAKE

Charlie and the Great Glass Elevator

The heroes of *Charlie and the Chocolate Factory* reappear in *Charlie and the Great Glass Elevator*. In the first book, the glass elevator carries visitors around the factory. Now, the elevator transports them much farther. Charlie, the entire Bucket family, and Willy Wonka travel somewhere extraordinary in this magical elevator—they blast off to outer space. The space crew faces marvelous adventures and meets some unusual characters. They even help return a lost American spaceship safely to Earth.

The BFG

The BFG is a story with a "big" surprise. When a giant steals young Sophie from her bedroom, she fears the worst. She assumes that the giant is going to eat her. The giant carries her off to Giant Country. To her surprise, the giant does not want to hurt Sophie. He is, after all, known as the BFG, or "Big Friendly Giant." Part of his job as the BFG involves dreams. He invents dreams, which he trumpets into children's rooms while they sleep. The BFG has to call upon his good powers, along with Sophie's talents, to stop the evil giants of the world.

AWARDS
The BFG
1986 International Board on Books for Young People Awards

Fantastic Mr. Fox

The book, *Fantastic Mr. Fox*, is a little different from some of Roald Dahl's other children's stories. The hero of this magical story is not a child, but an intelligent fox. Mr. Fox lives on a chicken farm that is owned by three nasty farmers—Boggis, Bunch, and Bean. The farmers try to force Mr. Fox and his family off their property. Mr. Fox outsmarts the three at every turn. By preventing the farmers from fulfilling their plans, clever Mr. Fox also helps the other animals on the farm.

Matilda

This book is about a bright, young girl who loves to read. However, Matilda's parents, do not care how intelligent she is. They think that she is a nuisance. To get her out of their way, Matilda's parents send her to Crunchem Hall School. The headmistress, Mrs. Trunchbull, is a cruel woman who hates children. She blames all wrongdoings on the well-meaning girl. Matilda quickly learns not to wear pigtails in order to avoid being flung around by them. During one of Mrs. Trunchbull's terrible outbursts, Matilda discovers her own incredible powers. She can make objects fly through the air. She uses her powers to punish her parents and the evil headmistress.

AWARDS
Matilda
1988 Federation of Children's Book Groups Award
1998 "Nation's Favorite Children's Book" in BBC Bookworm Poll

James and the Giant Peach

James Henry Trotter is very unhappy. Huge rhinoceroses escaped from the London Zoo and ate his parents. Now, James is stuck living with his two horrible aunts, Aunt Sponge and Aunt Spiker. James has no one to play with and nothing fun to do. When the fruitless fruit tree in the backyard suddenly grows a peach, James's life changes. The peach grows and grows until it is nearly as big as a house. James discovers a tunnel into the side of the peach. He climbs inside and moves toward the center of the fruit. There, he discovers giant, friendly insects. The peach rolls out of the garden, beginning a long journey for those on board. It barrels through the town and plunges into the sea. At sea, the crew's adventures take some exciting turns. James's humorous adventures are simply peachy.

Walt Disney Pictures adapted *James and the Giant Peach* into a stop-motion animation movie in 1996.

From Big Ideas to Books

Roald had written stories for adults for many years before he began writing children's books. Since Roald had already been published in many magazines, readers recognized his name. This recognition, along with his writing talent, made publishing his children's stories easier.

When *Charlie and the Chocolate Factory* was brought to bookstores in the United States, it sold 10,000 copies within the first month.

"It has been my good fortune as a writer that what I have wanted to write has for the most part proved to be saleable."
—*Roald Dahl*

A few years later, a Chinese edition of the book was published. Two million copies were printed. This was the greatest number of books ever to be printed at one time. Roald's books were **translated** and published in countries around the world, including Spain, Sweden, and Norway.

Some critics thought that *Charlie and the Chocolate Factory* was too violent for children. Roald's dedicated readers disagreed. Children loved the **gruesome** parts of his stories.

The Publishing Process

Publishing companies receive hundreds of **manuscripts** from authors each year. Only a few manuscripts become books. Publishers must be sure that a manuscript will sell many copies. As a result, publishers reject most of the manuscripts they receive. Once a manuscript has been accepted, it goes through

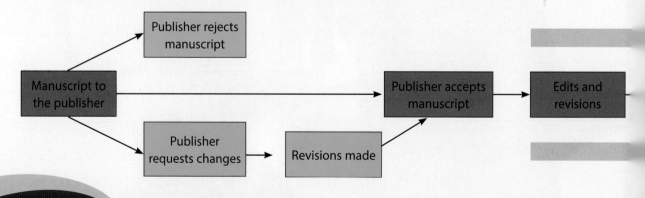

Roald's other books were just as successful as *Charlie and the Chocolate Factory*. Between 1980 and 1990, more than 11 million Roald Dahl books were sold in Britain. Roald's writing style and clever plots kept children interested in reading, and his books flew off the shelves. Roald spent nearly thirty years writing children's books.

Today, Roald Dahl's books remain a favorite among children. In 2000, he was awarded with the Millennium Children's Book Award. In the same year, *Charlie and the Chocolate Factory* was hailed the most important children's book published between 1960 and 1980. Roald Dahl's books have won awards in countries across the globe, including Australia, England, Holland, and the United States.

Roald wrote 19 books for young readers. His books have been translated into 34 languages.

many stages before it is published. Often, authors change their work to follow an editor's suggestions. Once the book is published, some authors receive royalties. This is money based on book sales.

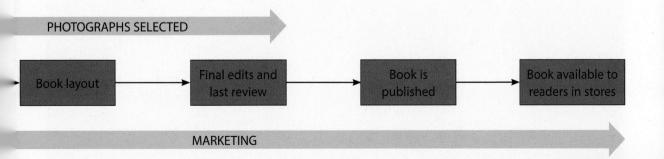

PHOTOGRAPHS SELECTED

Book layout → Final edits and last review → Book is published → Book available to readers in stores

MARKETING

Roald Dahl Today

Roald and Patricia were married for thirty years. They divorced in 1983. Roald spent the rest of his life married to another woman, Felicity Crosland. As children, Roald and Felicity had lived on the same block in Llandaff. They did not meet until 1972. Roald was a very productive author during the years he spent with Felicity. In the last two decades of his life, Roald wrote almost twenty books. Some of his most popular books, including *The BFG* and *Matilda*, were written during this period.

Although best known as an author, Roald was also a **philanthropist**. Throughout his life, he donated both time and money to many good causes. He wanted to help people in need. Roald visited hospitals to lift the spirits of people who were sick or dying. He was happy that his stories had the power to bring happiness to people's lives. Sadly, Roald himself became ill. He was **diagnosed** with a blood disease. He died on November 23, 1990 at 74 years of age.

Even though he died more than 20 years ago, people continue to remember Roald Dahl. and pay tribute to his legacy.

People everywhere mourned Roald's death. His fans were saddened by the loss of a great writer. Roald Dahl's readers continue to visit his grave in Buckinghamshire, England. They place trinkets and flowers on his grave to show their appreciation for his stories and his acts of kindness. Most often, his grave is covered with one of his favorite treats—chocolate.

Even after his death, Roald continued to help others. Most of his money was used to form the Roald Dahl Foundation. The foundation offers **grants** to individuals and institutions associated with literacy, **neurology**, and **hematology**. These areas affected Roald's life and the lives of those around him. He hoped that his money could be used to help people who are suffering.

Writing About the Person Today

The biography of any living person is an ongoing story. People have new ideas, start new projects, and deal with challenges. For their work to be meaningful, biographers must include up-to-date information about their subjects. Through research, biographers try to answer the following questions.

1 Has the person received awards or recognition for accomplishments?

2 What is the person's life's work?

3 How have the person's accomplishments served others?

Roald's books continue to capture the imaginations of children of all ages.

Fan Information

One of Roald Dahl's greatest accomplishments is that children and adults around the world still read his books. In England, Roald's books have sold about 30 million copies. His books are also bestsellers in the United States.

Movies, audio books, and plays also bring Roald's tales to life. The most popular movie, *Willy Wonka and the Chocolate Factory*, came to theaters in 1971. In 2005, a new film version of *Charlie and the Chocolate Factory* was released, starring Johnny Depp. Children still love to watch the antics of these entertaining characters on the big screen.

The Roald Dahl Children's Gallery in Buckinghamshire, England is home to a variety of imaginings from Roald's books, including Matilda's library, Mr. Fox's tunnel, and a Great Glass Elevator ride from *Charlie and the Great Glass Elevator*.

Matilda, Danny the Champion of the World, and *James and the Giant Peach* have also been made into movies. Several of Roald Dahl's books have also been adapted into plays, including *Matilda, James and the Giant Peach*, and *Charlie and the Chocolate Factory.* These stories continue to be told on stages around the world.

Ever since he wrote his first children's book, Roald Dahl has gained many devoted fans. Even after his death, Roald Dahl's fan base remains strong. The Internet is a great place to find websites devoted to Roald Dahl. To search, just type "Roald Dahl" into a search engine such as Google or Yahoo.

Publishers continue to keep Roald's characters alive. In 2011, a *Charlie and the Chocolate Factory* pop-up book was released, allowing readers to experience the story in a new way.

Write a Biography

A ll of the parts of a biography work together to tell the story of a person's life. Find out how these elements combine by writing a biography. Begin by choosing a person whose story fascinates you. You will have to research the person's life by using library books and reliable websites. You can also e-mail the person or write him or her a letter. The person might agree to answer your questions directly.

Use a concept web, such as the one below, to guide you in writing the biography. Answer each of the questions listed using the information you have gathered. Each heading on the concept web will form an important part of the person's story.

Parts of a Biography

Early Life

Where and when was the person born?

What is known about the person's family and friends?

Did the person grow up in unusual circumstances?

Growing Up

Who had the most influence on the person?

Did he or she receive assistance from others?

Did the person have a positive attitude?

Developing Skills

What was the person's education?

What was the person's first job or work experience?

What obstacles did the person overcome?

Person Today

Has the person received awards or recognition for accomplishments?

What is the person's life's work?

How have the person's accomplishments served others?

Early Achievements

What was the person's most important early success?

What processes does the person use in his or her work?

Which of the person's traits were most helpful in his or her work?

Test Yourself

1 Where was Roald Dahl born?

2 What was the name of Roald Dahl's mother?

3 Did Roald Dahl go to university or college after he finished high school?

4 Who did Roald Dahl meet in New York City and eventually marry?

5 What did Roald Dahl do during World War II?

6 Toward what good cause did much of Roald Dahl's money go?

7 During his lifetime, how many children's books did Roald Dahl write?

8 Where did Roald Dahl move to be close to a publishing center?

9 As an adult, where did Roald write his thoughts and ideas?

10 Approximately how many of Roald Dahl's books have been sold in England?

ANSWERS

1. Roald Dahl was born in Llandaff, Wales. 2. Sofie 3. Roald never went to university or college. He worked and traveled instead. 4. Patricia Neal, an American movie actress 5. Roald Dahl enlisted as a fighter pilot with the Royal Air Force. 6. The Roald Dahl Foundation. 7. Roald Dahl wrote 19 books. 8. New York City, New York. 9. Roald wrote his thoughts and ideas in a red notebook. 10. Approximately 30 million of Roald Dahl's books have been sold in England.

Writing Terms

The field of writing has its own language. Understanding some of the more common writing terms will allow you to discuss your ideas about books.

action: the moving events of a work of fiction

antagonist: the person in the story who opposes the main character

autobiography: a history of a person's life written by that person

biography: a written account of another person's life

character: a person in a story, poem, or play

climax: the most exciting moment or turning point in a story

episode: a scene or short piece of action in a story

fiction: stories about characters and events that are not real

foreshadow: hinting at something that is going to happen later in the book

imagery: a written description of a thing or idea that brings an image to mind

narrator: the speaker of the story who relates the events

nonfiction: writing that deals with real people and events

novel: published writing of considerable length that portrays characters within a story

plot: the order of events in a work of fiction

protagonist: the leading character of a story; often a likable character

resolution: the end of the story, when the conflict is settled

scene: a single episode in a story

setting: the place and time in which a work of fiction occurs

theme: an idea that runs throughout a work of fiction

Key Words

adapted: changed in order to make suitable

appendicitis: an illness characterized by swelling of the appendix

diagnosed: having the cause of symptoms identified, usually by a doctor

discriminating: having excellent taste or judgment

drafts: rough copies of something written

grants: money awarded for a specific reason or cause

gruesome: disgusting; creepy

hematology: the study of blood

manuscripts: drafts of stories before they are published

measles encephalitis: a virus that spreads to the brain, often causing death

mythology: a group or collection of stories or legends, often about gods and heroes

neurology: the branch of medicine dealing with the nervous system

philanthropist: a person who helps humankind through charitable actions or donations

pneumonia: an illness in which the lungs become congested

publication: to print for sale or distribution to the public

Swahili: a language spoken in Eastern and Central Africa

translated: rewritten in another language

vocabulary: all of the words used or understood by a person or group

Index

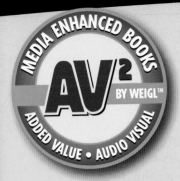

Log on to www.av2books.com

AV² by Weigl brings you media enhanced books that support active learning. Go to www.av2books.com, and enter the special code found on page 2 of this book. You will gain access to enriched and enhanced content that supplements and complements this book. Content includes video, audio, weblinks, quizzes, a slide show, and activities.

AV² Online Navigation

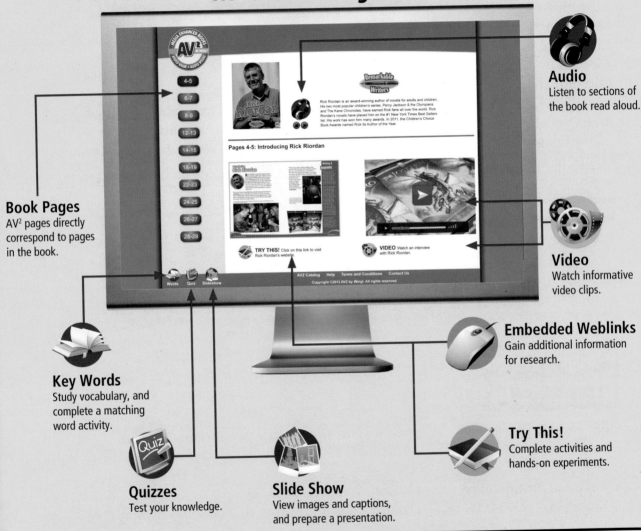

Audio
Listen to sections of the book read aloud.

Book Pages
AV² pages directly correspond to pages in the book.

Video
Watch informative video clips.

Embedded Weblinks
Gain additional information for research.

Key Words
Study vocabulary, and complete a matching word activity.

Try This!
Complete activities and hands-on experiments.

Quizzes
Test your knowledge.

Slide Show
View images and captions, and prepare a presentation.

AV² was built to bridge the gap between print and digital. We encourage you to tell us what you like and what you want to see in the future.

Sign up to be an AV² Ambassador at www.av2books.com/ambassador.

Due to the dynamic nature of the Internet, some of the URLs and activities provided as part of AV² by Weigl may have changed or ceased to exist. AV² by Weigl accepts no responsibility for any such changes. All media enhanced books are regularly monitored to update addresses and sites in a timely manner. Contact AV² by Weigl at 1-866-649-3445 or av2books@weigl.com with any questions, comments, or feedback.